CHRIST IN YOU, the Hope of Glory

RANDY CLARK

Edited by: Susan Thompson, Marion Hayes, and Bob Baynard

Apostolic Network of Global Awakening
1451 Clark Street
Mechanicsburg, PA 17055

For more information on how to order this book or any of the other materials that Global Awakening offers, please contact the Global Awakening Bookstore.

ISBN: 978-1-937467-71-5

Global Awakening
{ Core Message Series }

It is our desire to bring the messages of the Kingdom to the people of God. We have taken what we consider to be core messages from Randy Clark's sermons and schools and printed some of them in booklet form. We hope this teaching increases your understanding of God's purposes for the times we are in and that you find yourself encouraged in your faith. Other core messages are available and they are listed at the end of this booklet.

Table of Contents

{ Introduction }

In 2011, I was in Brazil with a Global Awakening mission team. We had been ministering in several churches in the São Paulo area and seen God moving in a mighty display of His glory as many were healed. A young woman came to one of the services in need of healing. She was in her twenties. Tall and slender, she was a classically trained dancer, but her career had been cut tragically short by an unfortunate accident. She had been riding on a scooter when one of her ankles became entangled in the spokes of the rear wheel resulting in a serious injury to the soft tissue. She sustained a huge gaping wound all the way to the bone, extending down the back of her leg to the base of her ankle. Doctors had been treating her for a year but were unsuccessful in bringing healing. She was facing amputation of part of her leg when she came to the healing service. With great expectation for healing she received prayer and God began to heal her. She had only been able to walk with crutches when she came to the service, but as God healed her ankle she was able to walk unassisted. Visible signs of healing were evident as the gaping hole in her leg began to close up. We were in awe at the glory of God on display that day.

The following December, in 2012, we were again in São Paulo with a mission team, ministering in the same church where this young woman had been healed the year before. Hearing that we were in town, she had made her way to the service. She let someone on our team know she was there and we brought her up on stage where she gave her testimony and showed us her ankle. Although a large scar remained, the huge wound in her ankle was healed. She finished sharing her testimony and then she began to dance. As she moved gracefully across the stage the glory of God fell in that church. Many of us could not remain standing in His presence.

This magnificent display of God's glory is only one of many that have shaped my understanding of the glory of God. When we embrace the ministry of healing, we can begin to understand more fully the love of our heavenly Father as He has displayed it in His Son Jesus. As we study glory together, it is my prayer that the Holy Spirit will create in you a new and greater hunger to press into the fullness of the knowledge of Christ in you, the hope of glory, so that you too may experience a greater empowering for His kingdom work, and come into the fullness of the knowledge of your identity in Christ.

We are a privileged people, and we must learn to fully engage this privilege we have been given. We must understand and embrace the reality that we are a priesthood of believers.[1] We are all priests under God. And make no mistake—the devil fights hard against the concept of the priesthood of believers. Because when we understand this concept, we can co-labor with Christ, with all His energy that works so mightily within us, to restore His kingdom here on earth.[2]

---

1. 1 Pet. 2:9.
2. 1 Cor. 3:9a, Col. 1:29, Matt. 6:10.

{ PART 1 }

UNDERSTANDING GLORY

The word glory is used in the Bible as a noun, a verb and an adjective. The Hebrew word for glory is "kabōd" and means abundance, honor, worth, and splendor.[3] In the Old Testament we find that the tent of meeting was sanctified by His glory (Exodus 29:43), and the temple was the place where His glory dwelled (Psalm 26:8). Isaiah says God has eyes of glory (Isaiah 3:8) and that the whole earth is full of His glory (Isaiah 6:3). The Psalmist exclaims that the heavens are declaring the glory of God (Psalm 19:2), and that He is the King of glory (Psalm 24:7-10). In the Old Testament we also read that the earth will be filled with a knowledge of the Lord (Habakkuk 2:14).

The Greek word for glory, *doxa*, has the meanings divine honor, divine splendor, and heavenly radiance; a state of being magnificent; greatness; a transcendent being deserving of honor; a majestic being (Acts 22:11, Luke 9:32).[4] In the New Testament we are told that everything in heaven has this radiance. The state of being in the next life is described as participation in the radiance of glory

---

3. Gerhard Kittel, *Theological Dictionary of the New Testament* (Grand Rapids, MI: Eerdmans Publishing, 1964), 2: 245.

4. Ibid., 2: 233-37.

(1 Corinthians 15:40-43). Cherubim, angels, and especially God himself are examples of the noun form of glory (Luke 2:9, Hebrews 9:5).

As I prepared this message on glory, it quickly became obvious that glory is a major theme of the Bible, and rightly so. As the people of God, we are called to give Him glory. In the context of the ministry of healing, we need look no further than Jesus' ministry as our example of how to do this. Through healings, miracles, signs and wonders, Jesus continually gave glory to His Father during His ministry on this earth. In the gospel of John, Jesus prays to his Father, "I have brought you glory on earth by finishing the work you gave me to do" (John 17:4). And He continues to do this as we minister in His name today. Glory is a favorite term of the apostle John. He depicts the whole life of Jesus as glorifying the Father.[5] At the same time John shows us how the Father glorifies the Son by the miracles He, the Father, has Jesus perform.[6]

This booklet is not an exhaustive study of glory in the Bible. I have been selective in the scriptures I have chosen to use focusing on the relationship of glory to healing and miracles because that is the arena God has called me into in the Church.

A BRIEF HISTORY OF CESSATIONIST THEOLOGY

The Roman Catholic Church has historically had a more biblical view of healing than many Protestant denominations. Believing that healings and miracles still occur today, the Roman Catholic Church holds to a "proof

5. John 12:28, 14:13, 17:4.
6. John 8:54, 13:31-32, 17:1.

of doctrinal orthodoxy" view, which says that the primary purpose of miracles is to evidence true doctrine. I disagree.

While the Catholic Church was saying, "miracles prove our doctrine," Protestants, in their quest for authority, threw out present-day miracles saying, "We do not need miracles because the real miracles that are authenticating doctrine are in the Bible. Once the Bible was canonized, the need for miracles ceased." To this Protestant way of thinking, a continuation of miracles would require new doctrine being added in the form of new scripture, creating a crisis of authority. The negative view of healing that we find in much of the Protestant Church today has emerged from this historical context. Although I understand the reasons why Luther and Calvin developed a low regard for healing and miracles, I do not agree with their positions. I do not believe that cessationist theology is the answer to the issue of authority.

I believe God gives miracles to accompany the preaching of the Gospel. Miracles are part of the Gospel. They are part of the good news that the Kingdom of God is at hand. For a more in-depth understanding of cessationist issues, I would recommend reading the contemporary writings of Dr. Jon Ruthven, Dr. Gary Greig, and Dr. Wayne Grudem, all of which give powerful biblical answers to cessationist theology.[7]

---

7. Jon Ruthven, *On the Cessation of the Charismata: The Protestant Polemic on Postbiblical Miracles* (Sheffield, UK: Sheffield Academic Press, 2011); Jon Ruthven, *What's Wrong With Protestant Theology? Traditions vs Biblical Emphasis* (Tulsa, OK: Word and Spirit Press, 2013); Gary S. Greig, "The Purpose of Signs and Wonders in the New Testament: What Terms for Miraculous Power Denote and Their Relationship to the Gospel," in Gary S. Greig and Kevin N. Springer, eds., *The Kingdom and the Power: Are Healing and the Spiritual Gifts Used*

Let's look more closely at the issue of authority, which is at the heart of the debate. The Roman Catholic Church was experiencing miracles and healings and therefore felt certain that God was authenticating their doctrine through these miraculous works. Luther, who had been trained as an Augustinian monk, also believed miracles were for the authentication of biblical doctrine. However, he was convinced that some of the doctrines and practices within the Roman Catholic Church were unbiblical. It followed then, that if the Roman Catholic Church had unbiblical doctrines and practices, then their miracles could not be authentic.

In sixteenth-century Germany, a religious sect emerged called Anabaptism. Anabaptism went beyond religion, spilling over into issues of liberty and justice, and it proposed industrial and political reform, but their ideas were rejected by the ruling nobility. A revolt of the peasants ensued. In the midst of this revolt, a fanatical Anabaptist, Thomas Müntzer, emerged. Müntzer claimed that he received divine prophetic revelation directly from God. His fanatical teachings, along with the influence of other leaders of the revolt, inflamed the country and before it was all over, more than one hundred thousand peasants were slain. Throughout it all Luther remained silent until Müntzer's influence began to cast a dark shadow on the Church. It was then that Luther felt compelled to make a determination on the issue of authority, declaring the Bible the only means of revelation, not miracles or prophecies. While Luther's reaction to the tragedy of the revolt is understandable, he essentially "threw the baby out with the bath water," relegating miracles to the early Church only.

---

by Jesus and the Early Church Meant for the Church Today? (Ventura, CA: Regal Books, 1993), 133-74; Wayne Grudem, "Should Christians Expect Miracles Today? Objections and Answers from the Bible," in Greig and Springer, eds., *The Kingdom and the Power*, 55-110.

Through Luther's writings we see that he favored the gospel of John more than the other three gospels because the book of John has only seven miracles, whereas Matthew, Mark, and Luke are full of miracles. Likewise, Luther gravitated to the epistles over the gospels because the epistles have fewer miracles. Yet, in all fairness to Luther, there is a degree of comfortableness with the miraculous in his ministry. His letter to a dying man proclaimed, "You will not die! You will outlive me because I have need of you." The man recovered from his deathbed and outlived Luther by a few days. He also prayed for a friend and co-reformer, Philipp Melanchthon, who was in a coma, close to death. Luther prayed a prayer of faith, laying hold of the promises of God. Philipp was healed.

Calvin's writings reveal an openness to the miraculous also, with limitations. He believed that when the Gospel was taken into places where it had never been heard, miracles could happen until the Church was established in that place. Once the Church was established, Calvin believed miracles would cease. This semi-cessationist theology essentially truncated the Gospel. With this brief history of cessationist theology in mind, let's turn our attention to the traditional interpretation of Colossians 1:25-29.

THE TRADITIONAL INTERPRETATION AND BEYOND

The traditional evangelical understanding of this passage is that the anointing of God, or God's Spirit in us, is our hope of glory in the future. When Christ returns, we will be given a glorified body and experience glory in the next life. This is the eschatological interpretation, and it is focused on the end times and on the second coming of Jesus.[8] I absolutely believe that the glory of God upon

8. Eschatology is a branch of theology concerned with the fi-

us and in us is our down payment, our guarantee, that in the end we will receive a glorified body in the general resurrection. And this is good news! Very good news. But, if we stop here, we will not grasp the fullness of this scripture; we will fail to understand what I believe is the main meaning of this passage.

It is important to keep in mind, that in mainline Protestantism; most of the promises of Scripture are to be found in the Millennium.[9] They are not for today. We are told that they will happen in the millennial reign of Christ that will commence with His second coming. This futuristic interpretation of Colossians 1:25-29 is the traditional interpretation.

I want to give you another way of looking at this passage, another interpretation; however, my interpretation is not the traditional one. While I believe the traditional interpretation has truth in it, I think it is insufficient to explain all that took place at the Cross and to capture the full meaning the apostle Paul intended when he wrote this passage. We need a bigger view, which comes when we remove the reformational lenses of Luther and Calvin and let the text speak for itself. Luther and Calvin were both reacting to Catholicism in the development of their doctrine. We must be mindful not to interpret Scripture through a reactionary lens.

Mind you, I am not throwing out the traditional interpretation, but adding to it. I do not stand alone in my interpretation. There are other theologians and scholars who agree with me.[10] Let's begin with the scripture itself.

---

nal events in the history of the world.

9. The Millennium is the 1,000-year period during which Christ will reign on the earth.

10. ". . . the evidence in Colossians, and in Pauline epistles,

I have become its [the Church's, the body of Christ's] servant by the commission God gave me to present to you the word of God in its fullness—the mystery that has been kept hidden for ages and generations, but is now disclosed to the saints. To them God has chosen to make known among the Gentiles the glorious riches of this mystery, which is Christ in you, the hope of glory.

Colossians 1:25-27

The concept of glory as it is found throughout most of the Bible is about more than the state of being glorified,

---

and throughout the Greek NT suggests that Col 1:27—"Christ in you, the hope of glory"—is not limited to referring to the state of our glorified bodies in the future, but it refers to a foretaste and experience of the glory and anointing of Christ in us now through the Holy Spirit." Dr. Gary Greig, e-mail message to me, September 11, 2013.

". . . Paul spells this out specifically: "the *glory*" is being revealed ***now** to the saints* "the riches of the glory of this mystery [which] is ***Christ in you"—Jesus' own person and mission—all that He is, right NOW*** . . . So to conclude, I think the use of terms for Christ's glory and His power naturally were understood in Pauline epistles and in the NT to include reference to healing and miracles as associated with His glory and presence through His Spirit in believers." Dr. Jon Ruthven, e-mail message to me, September 8, 2013.

"There is glory in God in Christ and in Christians and the glory in Christians is Christ in them, and this in turn is the hope of glory (Col 1:27). Christ's glory is given and will be fully given at the end of the world. Glory is thus in Paul an eschatological experience—i.e., it is a partly fulfilled reality, although it is also a future expectation into which we enter by degree (2 Cor. 3:18; cf. Rom. 9:23; 2 Thess. 2:14)." [From Keith R. Crim and George A. Buttrick, *The Interpreter's Dictionary of the Bible* (New York, NY: Abingdon Press, 1962), s.v. "Glory," by G. Henton Davies]." Dr. Andrew Park, e-mail message to me, September 13, 2013.

as in our "glorified bodies" that we will receive upon the second coming of Christ. If this were the only meaning of glory, then glory would only be available to us in the future, not in the present. And if glory is not available to us now, then the Gospel has no emphasis on healing or deliverance. Instead, the Gospel becomes like term life insurance—you have to die to get the benefits. If this were true, then it would follow that we have no hope in this world, only in the next.

Karl Marx, the founder of communism, dubbed Christianity the "opiate of the people," saying Christians preached "pie in the sky," rather than a hope for the present. That's the kind of thinking that can come out of the traditional interpretation of this passage.

When we look at the Cross through the lens that many Protestants use today in the twenty-first century, the predominant understanding of the death of Jesus is found in the doctrine of substitutionary atonement. "God made him who had no sin to be sin for us, so that in him we might become the righteousness of God."[11] Jesus is the substitute. He is the Lamb of God who was slain. He bore in His body our sins, our sicknesses, and our diseases. As the substitutionary atonement He died that we would not have to. The main understanding of the Cross, particularly for Protestants, is that Jesus' death allows us to get to heaven. He has unlocked the grave so that we may have eternal life.

This is wonderful news! I believe in the doctrine of substitutionary atonement. However, if we stop there, we fail to capture everything that the Cross represents. If we are to really capture everything that happened at the Cross, we need a bigger view. And to get to this bigger view, we must return

---

11. 2 Cor. 5:21.

to the understanding of the Cross from the first 1,000 years of the Church. What I am talking about here is a biblical, scriptural understanding of the Cross, which includes substitutionary atonement, *and* victory in the present life.

The primary emphasis of the Cross and what Jesus did on the Cross, for the first 1,000 years of the Church, is called Christus Victor. Christus Victor means this: Jesus died on the Cross, in our place. God raised Him from the dead and gave Him power over all powers. Because of His resurrection, He defeated the enemy and has now ascended to the Father's right hand. He has poured out the Holy Spirit on us, on all flesh.

In Jesus we have victory over disease, demons, and death, *in the present*. We do not have to die to receive the benefits of the Cross. These benefits are available to us right now while we are alive; to heal our bodies and to give us victory over demonic oppression. This was the teaching of the early Church. Christus Victor is not an "either/or," it is a "both/and" understanding. We do not need to choose between substitutionary atonement *or* Christus Victor. We are given both substitutionary atonement *and* Christus Victor. But that which was the predominant understanding of the early Church eventually became the secondary understanding. This switch occurred during the Protestant Reformation, and it arose out of the issue of authority associated with miracles, which, as we saw earlier, led to cessationist theology.

Cessationist theology, which claims that miracles and healings are not part of the Gospel, gives us, in essence, a gospel that is "not yet." However, Jesus announced the Gospel as the "good news" that the Kingdom of God has dawned.[12] He brought the Kingdom with Him, and he left it here. Nowhere does Jesus say that the Kingdom of God would leave when He left. In fact, He said the opposite. He tells all believers that they will do the things He has done and even greater things.[13]We are to continue the work of the Kingdom until Jesus returns. However, we know that this Kingdom is now only "in part." We will not see the fullness of the Kingdom until the second coming of Jesus. So we live in a Kingdom that is both "now" and "not yet."

This "now and not yet" aspect of the Kingdom explains why not all are healed, and why miracles sometimes do not occur. It also explains why present-day healings and miracles do occur. They back up the preaching of the Gospel. They are part of the "good news;" the good news that the power of the Holy Spirit is available because of the death, resurrection, and ascension of Jesus Christ. Now the precious Holy Spirit has been poured out, and healings and miracles can happen in the name of Jesus when the Gospel is faithfully preached; when the preachers believe that the message of the Gospel includes the in-breaking of the Kingdom of God as revealed in signs and wonders.

I think it is time that we, the Church, take off the glasses that gave us a sixteenth-century view so that we can see the bigger picture as it was seen by the early Church. It is this bigger picture that gives fullness to the meaning of Colossians 1:25-29. All of the benefits of the Cross are available to us now. We do not have to wait.

Some say this interpretation of Colossians is an over-realized eschatology—that I am expecting in the present those things that are reserved for the end times.

---

12. Mark 1:15.
13. John 14:12.

My response is: "No, I am not guilty of an over-realized eschatology. You are guilty of an under-realized present reality." The writer of Hebrews said that we were living in the last days ever since the coming of Jesus.[14]

THE NEW COVENANT FULFILLED

Let's examine the remainder of the Colossians passage, beginning at verse 28.

> *He is the one we proclaim, admonishing and teaching everyone with all wisdom, so that we may present everyone fully mature in Christ. To this end I strenuously contend with all the energy Christ so powerfully works in me.*
>
> ***Colossians 1:28-29***

The energy Paul is speaking of here is not the energy of God that is going to come and give us a glorified body at the end of time. Paul is talking about God's energy being available to us right now through the Holy Spirit. Just as Paul labored with God's energy working powerfully within him, we too can strenuously contend, right now, with all His energy that works so powerfully within us, as we co-labor with Christ.

The anointing of the Holy Spirit (God's energy) on us is the same anointing that was on Jesus during His time on earth. It is the same power that He operated in. Jesus tells us in John 16:5-16 that it was to our advantage that He went away. When He ascended to sit at the right hand of the Father, He was able to send the Holy Spirit, and it is the Holy Spirit, the Spirit of truth, who guides us in all truth, speaking not on His own, but only what He hears, bringing

14. Heb. 1:1-2.

glory to God. In this way Jesus comes back to us and is able to be with all of His people, everywhere, at all times.

The anointing of the Spirit is in us through the unity of the Trinity. Jesus Himself summarizes this revelation, this truth for us in the gospel of John, in chapters 14-16. He tells us that He and the Father are going to be in us, and that the Holy Spirit is going to be upon us. And because of this, we will bring glory to Jesus and to God. This revelation, this truth, is the hope of glory. This is the mystery that was hidden and has now been revealed—that the power of God is no longer just coming upon priests and kings and judges, but upon every believer in the New Covenant. The New Covenant is now being fulfilled in Jesus. The power of the Spirit is coming and He is on us now. The Kingdom of God can be advanced through you and me, and the gates of hell shall not prevail against us, the Church.

You have often heard the phrase, "The gates of hell." But just what are the gates of hell? As a kid I used to think that the Church was "here" and the gates of hell were "out there," and that the Church was in a defensive position. But I was a little country boy and I was wrong. That theology was wrong. I don't know where I got it. Maybe it had something to do with the preaching under which I grew up. But it is really the other way around. The devil does not have the advantage; the Church does, thanks to the finished work of Christ on the Cross. Jesus came and took the keys of the kingdom of this earth away from Satan and gave them to the Church. In the power of the risen Christ we, the Church, continually invade the kingdom of this world. With the energy of Jesus working so mightily within us, we heal the sick, cast out demons, raise the dead, and deliver people from the coming judgment of hell. The

Church is always busy decreasing the population of hell. The devil is the one on the defensive.

During World War II, between D-Day and VE-Day (Victory in Europe Day), there was a real battle going on, but the war had already been won on D-Day. In the same way, the Cross is D-Day. The war was won at the Cross and in Christ's resurrection. VE-Day will be when Jesus returns. The victory was ours when all the powers of hell could not hold Jesus in the grave and He was raised by the Father's good will. We live in this time of victory, even though the fighting will continue until the second coming of Christ.

In Colossians, Paul gives us a stunning picture of our victory and of Satan's defeat.

> *When you were dead in your sins and in the uncircumcision of your sinful nature, God made you alive with Christ. He forgave us all our sins, having canceled the written code, with its regulations, that was against us and that stood opposed to us; he took it away, nailing it to the cross. And having disarmed the powers and authorities, he made a public spectacle of them, triumphing over them by the cross.*
>
> ***Colossians 2:13-15***

In verse 15 Paul is describing something that would have been very familiar to any Roman citizen of the first century. Whenever a Roman general conquered another army, he would take the general of the defeated army, strip him of all his regalia and his clothes, tie the man behind his horse and lead him into town. This public spectacle of shame and triumph is a picture of what Jesus did to Satan through the Cross. The stunning imagery Paul is giving us here in Colossians is that of Satan, the defeated enemy, being dragged behind Jesus, our matchless King, as He rides triumphantly on His white horse.

The devil was defeated at the Cross; all his authority was stripped away. Jesus has all authority now. It is important that we understand that Satan has no authority. He has power, but no authority. He must submit to the authority of Jesus. The gospels are full of examples of Jesus exercising this authority over the demonic.[15] With Christ in us, we carry that same authority in the anointing of the Holy Spirit.

Because of this victory, Christ in you is the hope of glory. It is not just about a glorified body, about glory in the future, in the end times. This glory is also for now. And it is a synonym for power—the power of the Holy Spirit. The power of the Spirit in you is the hope you have of glory, of bringing glory to the Father and to the Son. It is the power by which the signs and wonders of God are displayed for His glory. When we take authority over the works of Satan in this world, we bring glory to God.

This hope of power is not our kind of hope. It is more than that—it is a foundation of certainty. Christ in you is the foundation of your certainty that there is going to be a demonstration of power in your life, which will bring glory to God. The good works that Jesus prepared beforehand are destined for me and for you. I may be saved by grace but I have been saved to perform and move in the works of God that He prepared for those who are going to be His children. So Christ in you, that anointing in you, is the basis of your hope.

---

15. In Mark 1:9-13, immediately after His baptism in the Jordan by John, Jesus exercises His authority over Satan for 40 days in the wilderness. Then, almost everywhere He goes, He confronts the demonic, exercising His authority and bringing healing. Here are some examples: Mark 1:21-28; Mark 5:1-43; Mark 9:14-29.

You are anointed and loaded for bear, and the enemy ought to be afraid of you rather than you being afraid of the enemy. You are a danger to the devil. This is why the devil fights against the concept of the priesthood of believers. He does not want us to fully understand that all of us are priests under God, that we are a holy nation, and that we all are anointed. That it is not just the preachers and apostles and pastors, but Christ in each believer is the hope of glory.

Paul does not say "Christ in the five-fold ministry." He says "Christ in you." Jesus did not say "anyone who is an apostle, anyone who is a prophet, anyone who is an evangelist, anyone who is a pastor and teacher, you will do what I have been doing and even greater things than these because I am going to the Father." He did not say that. Rather, He said, "Anyone who believes in me, greater things than these shall he do because I am going to the Father."[16]

Under the Old Covenant the Spirit did not fall and rest on all of God's people. Instead, the Spirit just rested on the judges, the kings, the priests and the prophets. Jesus, the New Covenant, came to die so that His Spirit could fall on all of us. He did not come to die just so we can go to heaven. That is wonderful but that is not all. Jesus came with a plan. He has a plan for a paradise here, and He has a plan for human beings to rule. He has a plan for us to exercise His authority. We, God's people, fell in Adam, but Jesus is going to reverse that and restore God's plan.

The Bible says that in the end times, the New Jerusalem, the heavenly city, will come down out of heaven to the earth.[17] In other words, we started in paradise, in the

---

16. John 14:12.
17. Rev. 21:2, 10.

Garden, and we will end in paradise. And that paradise is here when the lion and the lamb lie down together and the swords are beat into plowshares.[18] The restoration of all things by Jesus is our hope. And this hope is for the future *and* for the present. When we limit the understanding of the Gospel to the future, we are not appropriating all that is already ours in the present.

GLORY AND POWER

In the context of the ministry of healing in the Church, it is important that we understand the biblical meaning of glory and power, because some of the reasons given for a lack of healing have to do with a misunderstanding of these terms. Glory and power are often used synonymously in the Bible. They are often one and the same. We will examine this concept of glory and power more closely in Part II, but for now, let's look briefly at a few examples from the gospel of John and the writings of Paul.

"This, the first of his miraculous signs, Jesus performed at Cana in Galilee. He thus revealed his glory, and his disciples put their faith in him" (John 2:11).

"Then Jesus said, 'Did I not I tell you that if you believed, you would see the glory of God?'" (John 11:40). Jesus is speaking here of raising Lazarus from the dead.

In Romans 6:4 Paul states, "We were therefore buried with him through baptism into death in order that, just as Christ was raised from the dead through the glory of the Father, we too may live a new life."

---

18. Isa. 2:4.

"So will it be with the resurrection of the dead. The body that is sown is perishable, it is raised imperishable; it is sown in dishonor, it is raised in glory; it is sown in weakness, it is raised in power" (1 Corinthians 15:42-43). Here Paul uses glory and power side-by-side - raised in glory, raised in power. Jesus was raised from the dead by the glory of the Father.

"And we, who with unveiled faces all reflect the Lord's glory, are being transformed in his likeness with ever-increasing glory, which comes from the Lord, who is the Spirit" (2 Corinthians 3:18).

"But we have this treasure in jars of clay to show that this all-surpassing power is from God and not from us" (2 Corinthians 4:7).

One of the most frequent questions asked about healing is, "Why don't more people get healed?" While no one knows the answer, there are correlations between what we believe and healing. If we fail to understand and exercise the power available to us, how can we expect to see God's glory? If we embrace a cessationist theology that says miracles and healings ended when the Church was established, we tend to see few, if any, healings. But if we understand the privilege given to us by Christ on the Cross, and if we understand how to operate as a priesthood of believers, empowered by the Spirit to do what Jesus did and even greater things than He did, then we see more healings. We see God glorified!

Remember the story of the Syrophoenician woman? It is found in both the gospel of Mark (Mark 7:25-30) and in Matthew (Matthew 15:21-28). This woman is a Gentile. Jesus had told His followers not to go to the Gentiles but to go into the lost house of Israel until the resurrection, when the power of the Spirit would be poured out. So here is a Syrophoenician woman, a Gentile, who comes to Jesus and says that her daughter needs to be delivered. Jesus responds by saying something unusual. He says, ". . . it is not right to take the children's bread and toss it to their dogs" (Mark 7:27). The Jews often referred to Gentiles as dogs. It was a very derogatory term. Today Jesus would be censured for that. But when Jesus said this to the Syrophoenician woman, He was essentially asking her, "How badly do you want this?"

But when we look more closely at this passage, there is something more here that Jesus is saying. When He says, "It's not right to take the children's bread," what did He mean? What is the children's bread in this instance; what did the daughter need? The answer is deliverance. Jesus is referring to deliverance as the children's bread in this passage. He is saying it is not right to take the ministry of deliverance [the children's bread], and give it to someone outside the covenant of God [the Gentiles or the dogs].

The woman's answer to Jesus' question reveals her faith. She says, "Yes, Lord, . . . but even the dogs under the table eat the children's crumbs" (Mark 7:28). Jesus, so impressed with her response and never having seen faith like this, heals her daughter. That which was reserved for the dispensation of the Gentiles, that was not even for the time this woman and her daughter were in, was given to her because of her act of faith. She was able to reach out and bring into her reality something God had reserved for the future. Her faith was so great that she was not willing to embrace an under-realized present reality. As a result, she was able to receive in the present what was reserved for the future.

Charles Finney was a man of great faith. He had so much faith for revival that it would literally break out in churches when he visited. Even though many of these churches had prayed for revival, they had not had faith for it to come, and it did not come until Finney, a man of faith, arrived. It is important to understand that great faith is not "the answer" in the ministry of healing unless that great faith is accompanied by an expectation (a focus) and an understanding of the will of God that healing is not to be a rare exception to the will of God but the natural display of His glory.

The same applies to healings, miracles, signs and wonders. We can be strong in faith and yet not see healing because we need to have faith for healing. We need to understand that the anointing can bubble up in us even when we are not yet strong in faith, because the one inside of us, Jesus, has great faith. And sometimes, when that bubbling up happens, we still tend to doubt, wondering and questioning if it is really God. We get into little wrestling matches, little battles, in which our little faith tries to pull down the faith of Christ in us. My advice is to forget the battle and just go with Jesus. He is in us, and He is mighty to save.

COOPERATING WITH THE PRESENCE OF GOD

In order to fully understand glory, I believe we must also understand the ways of God—how He creates faith in His people. In the book of Exodus, God gives us an illustration of His ways:

> *The LORD would speak to Moses face to face, as a man speaks with his friend. Then Moses would return to the camp, but his young aide Joshua son of Nun did not leave*

the tent. Moses said to the LORD, "You have been telling me, 'Lead these people,' but you have not let me know whom you will send with me. You have said, 'I know you by name and you have found favor with me.' If you are pleased with me, teach me your ways so I may know you and continue to find favor with you. Remember that this nation is your people." The Lord replied, "My Presence will go with you, and I will give you rest." Then Moses said to him, "If your Presence does not go with us, do not send us up from here. How will anyone know that you are pleased with me and with your people unless you go with us? What else will distinguish me and your people from all the other people on the face of the earth?" And the LORD said to Moses, "I will do the very thing you have asked, because I am pleased with you and I know you by name." Then Moses said, "Now show me your glory."

Exodus 33:11-18

Moses understood the importance of being taught by God in order to know Him and find favor with Him. We find an important insight in God's response to Moses. He tells Moses that His presence will go with him and that he will find rest. When we cooperate with the presence of God ministry moves from laboring and striving to a place of rest. The promises of God do not pose a problem for us to achieve, but are a promise to be received.[19]

---

19. I learned this expression "not a problem to be achieved, but a promise to be received" from Leif Hetland, a powerful apostolic evangelist among the Muslims of Pakistan.

What can be learned from this dialogue between Moses and God? First, learning the ways of God depends upon the presence of God, not on reducing our relationship with Him to principles or precepts. Second, Moses understood that learning the ways of God was key to knowing God and finding favor with Him. Moses not only wanted to know God's ways and to know Him better, and thus find favor; he also wanted to see God's glory. And lastly, although we will not find it in this particular passage, from a study of God's glory we learn that the primary way God revealed His glory in the Bible was through signs, wonders, healings, and miracles.[20]

This connection between learning the ways of God and the glory of God is very strong. Without learning the ways of God we will find it difficult to co-labor with Him. We will miss His leadings and will not experience the same level of faith that comes from knowing His will in a particular situation. When we know the will of God, we can have greater faith that God will respond to our prayers of command. Because we know that what we are commanding is His will as revealed through His revelatory gifts.[21]

It was John Wimber and Omar Cabrera who were most instrumental in helping me discover the ways of God regarding revelatory gifts – how they can occur, how to instruct the crowds to build their faith by teaching people the relationship between gifts of revelation and gifts of

---

20. Randy Clark, *Empowered: A School of Healing and Impartation Workbook* (Mechanicsburg, PA: Global Awakening, 2012), 191-204.

21. "This is the confidence we have in approaching God: that if we ask anything according to his will, he hears us. And if we know that he hears us—whatever we ask—we know that we have what we asked of him" (1 John 5:14-15).

power.[22] Omar also taught me about the importance of understanding the role of the angelic realm in healing. Through him I learned the importance of asking God to send angels into our meetings, as well as how the angelic can manifest to us, and how to interpret what we see. It was in this way that God created the faith in Omar to see the greatest miracles in his crusades.

It was John Wimber who taught me how to recognize words of knowledge. I was able to shadow him from 1984 to 1985, during his meetings in the U.S., and learn how to recognize signs of God's presence.

Through my study of the Word and through relationships with giants of the faith like Omar Cabrera and John Wimber, I have been privileged to gain insights into how gifts, faith, and healing and miracles are related. These insights have also come from forty-three years of experience in ministry, with thirty years of actively praying for the sick. I have been blessed to work on occasion with more than ten ministers who are all noted for their ministry of healing.[23] During these years of ministering to thousands of people in several thousand meetings, I have noticed the connection between healing and faith, and the connection between faith and revelatory gifts. With few exceptions, most of the miraculous healings involved a gift of faith, and this gift of faith was almost always the result of a revelatory gift. Even when it seemed as if no gift - such as a word of

---

22. The gifts of revelation are words of knowledge, words of wisdom, and discerning of spirits; the gifts of power are healings, faith, and working of miracles. The category not mentioned are the gifts of speech: tongues, interpretation of tongues, and prophecy.

23. These healing ministers include Heidi Baker, Bill Johnson, James Maloney, Omar Cabrera, Carlos Annacondia, Leif Hetland, Henry Madava, Cal Pierce, Ian Andrews, Jim and Ramona Rickard, James Maloney, and Todd White.

knowledge or a prophecy occurred - there was still the *still small voice* or impression, instructing the person praying or the one being prayed for.

SOVEREIGNTY, HOLINESS, AND POWER IN THE MINISTRY OF HEALING

Some attribute the lack of healings to the sovereignty of God, but I think an overemphasis on sovereignty is an insufficient explanation. People with a great healing anointing see more healings than others, which indicates to me that it is not just sovereignty at play in healing.

In the 1800s, when the Protestant Church began to recapture the understanding that healing is part of the promises of God and in the atonement, they began to see more healings than had been seen up to that point. I believe that it is more our expectation for healing than the sovereignty of God that affects healing. And it is an understanding of the atonement, an understanding of the Cross, which allows us to recapture the biblical basis for healing. Maria Woodworth-Etter, John G. Lake, Smith Wigglesworth, Oral Roberts, and others who believed in healings, saw more healings than ministers who did not believe healing was for today or in the atonement. It was not sovereignty that determined the numbers of healings; it was what people believed that determined the numbers of healings they saw in their meetings. I do not mean to imply that this is the only reason. There are other factors at play, such as anointing, gifting, the faith of the person being prayed for, and the expectation for healing in the congregation.

Now I believe that sometimes, God, in His sovereignty does not heal. There is a tension that exists, but I have to ask, "Does sovereignty have to make God a Grinch?" I don't think so. We have overused sovereignty to the point that God is portrayed as tight-fisted God who is hard to get anything out of. But it is really the other way around: we have a God who loves to give good gifts to His children; a God who sent His son to die on the Cross where He bore our sicknesses and diseases; a God who moves in power to heal through the finished work of Christ on the Cross.[24]

A misunderstanding of holiness has also influenced the flow of healing in the Church, especially the Catholic Church. Holiness in the Catholic Church was relegated to the domain of the priests and nuns who were deemed the only ones "holy enough" to minister healing. It was determined that the lay person, the "little old me's," because they lacked the necessary commitment displayed by the clergy, could not be used by God to minister healing.

This concept of holiness or lack thereof was taken to its extreme in the Middles Ages when those who moved in the gifts of prophecy or words of knowledge were burned at the stake as witches. At this point in history, the Church understood that the occult had power, and therefore anyone displaying power that was not a holy priest or nun had to be evil.

With ministry relegated exclusively to the clergy, demonstrations of miracles, healings, signs and wonders flowed only from those deemed saintly and holy. This led to the canonization of saints. Now the laity was instructed to pray to the saints who would then work miracles for them. The laity was caught in a double bind. People no longer believed that their prayers for healing would be

24. Isa. 53:4-5.

heard because they were not holy enough, and so they did not pray for healing. This misunderstanding of holiness that affected the flow of healing in the Church is a strategy of the enemy to keep people from understanding that God can use them, and that Christ in us is the hope of glory; the hope of the demonstration of healing, miracles, signs, and wonders.

And then there are those who believe that healings do not occur because God runs out of power. Have you ever heard anyone say, "Well, I'd like to be healed but the needs of others are so much greater than mine that I don't want you to pray for me. My need for healing is small compared to the needs of others, so pray for them instead." In other words, God is going to run out of power. He's going to go broke at some point. What kind of a God are we thinking about who does not have enough power to heal both the big physical problems and the small ones as well?

PERSEVERING GRACE THAT COMES FROM THE ANOINTING OF THE SPIRIT

In 1830, in response to the severe anti-Catholic sentiment prevalent at the time, a French Jesuit priest penned a little book that brought about a new teaching in the Church in America. This new teaching became what we call pre-trib, rapture, pre-millennial eschatology. It cannot be found in the history of the Church prior to 1830. Scofield included it in the notes of his Scofield Bible, and it became *the* major view of the Evangelical Church in America. It became a sacred cow. We boldly proclaim a "come to Jesus and get saved and you won't have to go through the tribulation" message. While there is comfort to be found in pre-trib, pre-millennial eschatology, it leaves believers unprepared when tribulation does come. This pre-trib, pre-millennial eschatology was taught to the Chinese Christians, who fell away from the Lord when persecution came because their faith had not prepared them for tribulation. Those who were able to persevere became filled with the Spirit.

Why should we be the only part of the Church that never has to go through any tribulation? There have been more Christians in the last hundred years or even the last twenty-five years that have died for the faith than in the first three hundred years of the Church. What we need is Christ in us, the hope of glory. We need the fullness of the Holy Spirit to be faithful to God when we experience trials. We need the reality of Christ in us, the hope of glory, so we don't buckle when all hell breaks loose and persecution comes against us. We need the persevering grace that comes from the anointing of the Spirit upon us.

UNDERSTANDING WHO WE ARE IN CHRIST

We need to come into the fullness of the understanding that we have something greater in us than outward holiness. We have the anointing of the Holy Spirit *in* our life. And we do not have to be perfect to be used by God, because the perfect One, Christ, who lives in us, is the one that can use us. We need to *believe* that Christ in us is the hope of glory. And this glory is not just for the future when we die. It is for the future *and* for now.

The Lord's Prayer is in part a warfare prayer. When Jesus tells us to pray, "Our Father who art in heaven, hallowed be thy name, thy kingdom come, thy will be done on earth as it is in heaven," He is teaching us to pray for the kingdom of God to come against the kingdom of this world. This is God's desire. Instead of praying that we can get out of the earth and into heaven, we should be praying that heaven comes to earth in us. Because the power of heaven is in us through the finished work of Jesus on the Cross, and it defeats the enemy.

In AD 595, Pope Gregory sent Augustine, prior of the Abbey of St. Andrew's in Rome, to Kent England to convert the Anglo-Saxons to Christianity. These Anglo-Saxons were composed of pagan tribes, among them the Picts and the Druids, who were very demonized people groups. This mission, known as the Gregorian Mission, was quite successful, with Augustine baptizing thousands one Christmas Day much like the mass baptisms of New Testament times. Augustine was not successful because of good preaching or teaching, but because the power of God was demonstrated to be greater than the power of the occult.

These pagan people groups practiced witchcraft and magic, and they understood the significance and power of occult spells and curses. In the occult realm, if someone works a pact or a covenant that has the power to bring you into bondage, you must then find a more powerful witch or warlock who can work a more powerful pact in order to break the existing pact or covenant that was placed on you. You can be freed from one bondage only to come under a stronger bondage. It is all about who has the most power.

The New Covenant, in the blood of Jesus, is more powerful than any other power. When these pagan people groups were confronted with the power of God in Christ Jesus, they converted by the thousands. In the gospels we see the power and authority of Jesus over the demonic realm.

> *And there was in their synagogue a man who had in him an unclean spirit; and he cried out saying, Jesus of Nazareth, what have we in common? Have you come to destroy us? I know who you are, Holy One of God. And Jesus rebuked him, saying, Be silent and come out of him. And the unclean spirit threw him down and cried out in a loud voice and left him. And they were all astonished, and kept asking one another, saying, What does this mean and what is this new teaching, that with such a power he commands even unclean spirits and they obey him?*
>
> ***Mark 1:23-27, Holy Bible from the Ancient Eastern Text***

In Mark 1:34 and again in Mark 3:11-12, we see Jesus addressing the demons and forbidding them to give witness to who He [Jesus] was. The ancient Eastern Aramaic translation of Mark 1:34 says that Jesus would not allow the demons to speak "because some of them were his acquaintances." Before Satan and his demons were cast out of heaven, they were in fellowship with Jesus in heaven while they were still angels. The demonic realm submits to Jesus' authority because they know Him as the Holy One of God, the Son of God. They know who He is!

> *And those who were afflicted with unclean spirits, when they saw him, fell down before him and cried, saying, You are indeed the Son of God. And he cautioned them earnestly not to make him known.*
>
> ***Mark 3:11-12, Holy Bible from the Ancient Eastern Text***

If the demonic realm knows and understands the power and authority of Jesus, should not we, His people, also understand who He is and live in the reality of the privilege given to us through His finished work on the Cross? We have been given a privilege, and we must recover the emphasis on our privilege, of who we are; that we are a people of faith; that we have faith that the Spirit in us is the hope of bringing glory to God. When we understand our identity in Christ, we can be used mightily by God to advance His Kingdom.

Every Christian has the anointing of Christ within them. We are loaded for ministry, loaded for glory and destined for glory. I believe it is the Lord's will for His people to understand this destiny. Ours is not a destiny of defeat and shame but a destiny of glory. Jesus wants us to bear much fruit and to see much glory. In John 14-16, when Jesus talks about fruit, He is talking about asking the Father for things: "even greater things than these, because I am going to the Father."[25] "Until now you have not asked for anything in my name. Ask and you will receive, and your joy will be complete."[26] Jesus wants us to bring glory to His Father by what we do.[27]

We are to co-labor with Christ. "For we are God's fellow workers; you are God's field, God's building" (1 Corinthians 3:9). Co-laboring with God is not something we do of ourselves. We are not channeling universal energy from the oneness of the understanding of god held by the New Age, New Thought, Theosophy, or Pantheism. Neither is this energy we are speaking of synonymous to other energy concepts, such as the Chinese 'chi,' Japanese 'ki,' Indian 'prana,' or Norse Odic force. We are not working with an impersonal

25. John 14:12.
26. John 16:24.
27. John 15:8.

energy force, which is subject to our control or our ability to channel. Instead, we are fellow workers with the Holy Spirit. We are working with a personal God through the personal Holy Spirit.[28] When we minister, we are to minister with the energy of God, the power of God. This is the will of God. It is our inheritance and our destiny. We need to meditate upon 2 Corinthians 4 and John 16 until these scriptures take root in us.

> *"It is written: 'I believed; therefore I have spoken.' With that same spirit of faith we also believe and therefore speak"*
>
> ***2 Corinthians 4:13***

> *"'All that belongs to the Father is mine. That is why I said the Spirit will take from what is mine and make it known to you'"*
>
> ***John 16:15***

It is the revelation that comes out of our relationship with God that gives us the faith to seek what we think God is saying in any given situation. And this is where the finished work of Christ on the Cross comes into its proper position. We can now boldly approach the throne of grace in our time of need because of what Jesus has already done.[29] We are seated with Christ in heavenly places. He

---

28. For a more in-depth understanding of occult energy and impersonal energy versus the energy of God through the Holy Spirit see the book I co-authored with Susan Thompson titled *Healing Energy: Whose Energy Is It?* (Mechanicsburg, PA: Global Awakening, 2013).

29. We live in a time where there is great confusion regarding the doctrine of the finished work. Some say it means we don't have to confess our sins anymore—doing so would indicate a lack of faith in the finished work. There are many scriptures that contradict this incor-

has given us authority. We are to come boldly on the basis of what He did, not our own performance.[30] This access to the throne room is the key to our understanding of the finished work of the Cross. He has made each of us holy. But to keep this in balance, we need to work out that salvation with fear and trembling.[31] It is by grace, but we have the responsibility to walk in relationship with Him, working out all that this relationship means.[32]

---

rect understanding of the finished work. One such passage is Hebrews 10, which illustrates why we can approach the throne of God with boldness, and it also shows us that we are not to take this faith in the finished work as a pretext to sin. It shows us that there is a responsibility to remain faithful and not to take the work of Jesus as a 'carte blanche' excuse to continue living a lifestyle of sin. I encourage you to read Hebrews chapter 10 so that you can see these dual truths for yourself, and see that though God is love and is good, He is still holy and requires us to live our lives in the power of the Spirit, in holiness.

30. Heb. 10:19.

31. "Therefore, my dear friends, as you have always obeyed—not only in my presence, but now much more in my absence—continue to work out your salvation with fear and trembling" (Phil. 2:12).

32. "For it is by grace you have been saved, through faith—and this not from yourselves, it is the gift of God— not by works, so that no one can boast. For we are God's workmanship, created in Christ Jesus to do good works, which God prepared in advance for us to do" (Eph. 2:8-10). In these verses Paul makes very clear not only salvation by grace, but the concept that we were saved or created in Christ Jesus to do good works, which God prepared in advance for us to do. This is not a cheap grace, neither is regeneration a mere imputed righteousness, but is also an imparted righteousness. If we lose this biblical balance, we distort the biblical understanding of God. The holiness of God is revealed in His judgments, and it is against this backdrop of judgment that mercy and grace is expressed out of the love of God. This helps us to understand another passage where fear and trembling is mentioned, but this time at the time of conversion: "And his affection for you is all the greater when he remembers that you were all obedient, receiving him with fear and trembling" (2 Cor. 7:15).

My desire is that I want to experience Him and I want Him to see me as He says I am. I want to become so free that I can do everything that Jesus wants and I can confess what He says about me. That is the freedom I am looking for. That is what I believe the finished work is—a boldness to come on the basis of what Jesus did; not abusing His grace or His teaching, or removing everything else that Scripture teaches about the importance of utilizing our Advocate by confessing our sins.[33] I am not talking about a license to sin. I am talking about living in the finished work of Christ on the Cross, living with boldness in this reality, and of being able to approach the throne of grace to obtain help, power, grace-gifts and forgiveness.

---

33. Cf. 1 John 1:5-2:6. Some today are teaching that this passage was not written to the Church, but was written to the Gnostics. This is definitely not the case. While Gnosticism is dealt with in 1 John, the letter is written to the Church, not the Gnostics. The passage makes clear the need to continue to walk in holiness for those who have experienced the finished work, and when they sin, to confess their sins. Failure to do so is to hurt the relationship they have with God. Moreover, to purposefully continue living in sin and darkness proves they did not have a true salvation where the *Holy* Spirit came into their lives to conform them to Christ.

{ PART 2 }

THE RELATIONSHIP OF GLORY TO HEALINGS AND MIRACLES AS SEEN IN THE LAW AND THE PROPHETS

The relationship of glory to healings and miracles can be found in both the Old Testament as seen in the Law and the prophets, and in the New Testament as seen in the gospels. Let's first look at this relationship as it is found in the Old Testament. One of the ways in which God reveals His glory is through His provision. In Exodus we see God's miraculous provision for the Israelites:

> *So Moses and Aaron said to all the Israelites, "In the evening you will know that it was the Lord who brought you out of Egypt, and in the morning you will see the glory of the Lord, because he has heard your grumbling against him. Who are we that you should grumble against us?" Moses also said, "You will know that it was the Lord when he gives you meat to eat in the evening and all the bread you want in the morning, because he has heard your grumbling against him. Who are we? You are not grumbling against us, but against the Lord."*

> *Then Moses told Aaron, "Say to the entire Israelite community, 'Come before the Lord, for he has heard your grumbling.'"*
>
> *While Aaron was speaking to the whole Israelite community, they looked toward the desert, and there was the glory of the Lord appearing in the cloud. The Lord said to Moses, "I have heard the grumbling of the Israelites. Tell them, 'At twilight you will eat meat, and in the morning you will be filled with bread. Then you will know that I am the Lord your God.'"*[34]
>
> *That evening quail came and covered the camp, and in the morning there was a layer of dew around the camp. When the dew was gone, thin flakes like frost on the ground appeared on the desert floor.*
>
> **Exodus 16:6-14**

Moses tells the Israelites that they will see God's glory in His provision of bread (manna) to eat. Each morning, for forty years, manna appears on the ground to feed them. This miraculous provision was a manifestation of God's glory. God not only gave them bread to

---

34. Every time this sentence is recorded in the Old Testament, it is connected to God working a miracle or displaying His power. Dr. Jon Ruthven makes this point in his book, *What's Wrong With Protestant Theology.* Ruthven's research reveals that out of 134 cases that investigated the cause of the response "then they will know that I am God" in the Old Testament, it is always connected to God having revealed His power. This is the *characteristic way* that God reveals Himself (cf. Heb. 2:4; Rom. 15:19). See Ruthven, *What's Wrong,* 137n5.

eat, but He gave quail for meat in the evening, and water to drink supernaturally from a rock.

> *Moses and Aaron went from the assembly to the entrance to the Tent of Meeting and fell facedown, and the glory of the Lord appeared to them. The Lord said to Moses, "Take the staff, and you and your brother Aaron gather the assembly together. Speak to that rock before their eyes and it will pour out its water. You will bring water out of the rock for the community so they and their livestock can drink." So Moses took the staff from the Lord's presence, just as he commanded him. He and Aaron gathered the assembly together in front of the rock and Moses said to them, "Listen, you rebels, must we bring you water out of this rock?" Then Moses raised his arm and struck the rock twice with his staff. Water gushed out, and the community and their livestock drank.*
>
> ***Numbers 20: 6-11***

Under the Old Covenant we see God's compassion followed by demonstrations of His power. This is a reflection of God's true character. He is a God of mercy and compassion, and He desires to touch His people. When we ask for the compassion of God we will receive it. For God to do otherwise would be cruel and outside of His nature.

The prophet Isaiah tells us that when we minister to the poor, God's glory will be revealed.

> *Is not this the kind of fasting I have chosen: to loose the chains of injustice and untie the*

cords of the yoke, to set the oppressed free and break every yoke? Is it not to share your food with the hungry and to provide the poor wanderer with shelter - when you see the naked, to clothe them, and not to turn away from your own flesh and blood? Then your light will break forth like the dawn, and your healing will quickly appear; then your righteousness will go before you, and the glory of the Lord will be your rear guard. Then you will call, and the Lord will answer; you will cry for help, and he will say: Here am I. If you do away with the yoke of oppression, with the pointing finger and malicious talk, and if you spend yourselves in behalf of the hungry and satisfy the needs of the oppressed, then your light will rise in the darkness, and your night will become like the noonday. The Lord will guide you always; he will satisfy your needs in a sun-scorched land and will strengthen your frame. You will be like a well-watered garden, like a spring whose waters never fail. Your people will rebuild the ancient ruins and will raise up the age-old foundations; you will be called Repairer of Broken Walls, Restorer of Streets with Dwellings.

Isaiah 58:6-12

If we will spend ourselves on behalf of the poor, feeding the hungry, clothing the naked, and sheltering the homeless, God says that our light will rise in the darkness and our night will become like noonday. His glory will be revealed through us as we minister in His name.

A current-day demonstration of this promise of God has been seen repeatedly in the ministry of Rolland and Heidi Baker. Through Iris Ministries they care for thousands of men, women and children in Mozambique. On several occasions they have experienced a multiplication of food as they fed the multitudes.

In the New Testament, under the New Covenant, God's compassion is followed by demonstrations of His power through healings, miracles, signs and wonders. These are part of the Gospel. They are expressions of the Gospel. Healings, miracles, signs and wonders do not just testify to the Gospel but are an integral part of it. God the Father and the Son are glorified through miracles and healings.

I emphasize healings and miracles because I want God to receive glory. I do not just want to see His glory; I want Him to *receive* glory. The life and ministry of Jesus was all about the Father receiving glory.[35] And we are to continue the ministry of Jesus in the power of the Holy Spirit, giving glory to God. It is not a selfish thing to ask

---

35. "He who speaks on his own authority seeks his own glory; but he who seeks the glory of him who sent him is true, and in him there is no falsehood" (John 7:18, RSV). "When he heard this, Jesus said, 'This sickness will not end in death. No, it is for God's glory so that God's Son may be glorified through it'" (John 11:4). "Jesus said to her, 'Did I not tell you that if you would believe, you will see the glory of God?'" (John 11:40, ESV). "Jesus replied, 'The hour has come for the Son of Man to be ***glorified***.'" (John 12:23). "'Father, ***glorify*** your name!' Then a voice came from heaven, 'I have glorified it, and will glorify it again'" (John 12:28). "When he was gone, Jesus said, 'Now is the Son of Man glorified and God is glorified in him. If God is glorified in him, God will glorify the Son in himself, and will glorify him at once'" (John 13:31-32). "After Jesus said this, he looked toward heaven and prayed: 'Father, the hour has come. ***Glorify*** your Son, that your Son may ***glorify*** you'" (John 17:1).

for the glory of God; to ask to see people healed. Some people say healing ministry seems selfish to them, as if all the focus is on the ministry team. That is not true. It is not about the ministry team. It is about God receiving glory as He heals and delivers His beloved children.

In the early days of the Azusa Street Revival, they would tell people that God wanted to show His glory; that God wanted to do something to reveal His glory. They believed that the outpouring of the Spirit was to bring glory to God. I believe that too.

When we sing the words "Glorify Thy name, glorify Thy name, glorify Thy name in all the earth," do we understand what we are asking God to do? From a biblical perspective we are literally asking God to glorify His name. But a lot of us in the Church, when we sing that old song, do not have faith that God is actually going to show His glory. I would like to see us, the Church, sing from our heart with an expectation that says, "God, we really do want You to receive glory. We really do want to see You glorify Your name!"

In our work with the poor in St. Louis, and with Rolland and Heidi Baker in Mozambique, we have seen that when our expectation for God to reveal His glory is high, we see Him move in glory. When I pastored a church in St. Louis in the 1990s, we would deliver food into the poorest areas of the inner city. We did not just want to donate food to a food bank. Donating food to a food bank is a good thing to do, but we wanted to take the food directly to people in order to have opportunities to minister to them. Some people told us it was too risky, but we never felt unsafe. We made friends with the people we ministered to. In the privacy of their own homes, they would open up to us, disclosing their problems, and we would pray for them. We saw more miracles take place among the poor in St. Louis than anywhere else. The light of Christ rose in us in the midst of the darkness and shone like noonday. God showed His glory.

Once when I was ministering in South Carolina, an atmosphere of oppression came over the meeting. There were almost four hundred people present but only four were healed despite many words of knowledge. I felt anger rising in me and I stood up and said, "This will not do! This is not good enough! God does not get glory when only four people out of four hundred are healed. I am expectant for at least ten percent of you to be healed tonight. We cannot quit. We have to press through this. We are going for it!" At that point more words of knowledge came forth and faith began to rise. As we prayed, people began to get healed. Before the night was over, we had eighty people healed. Understand, I was thankful for the four people who were healed, but I knew that what was happening was not worthy of God. He deserved much more glory than just four healings.

HOW CONCERNED ARE WE FOR THE GLORY OF GOD?

I want to challenge every one of you, especially every pastor reading this, and ask you, "How concerned are you for the glory of God?" Pastors, hear me: it is not about how good our sermons are. It is not about how beautiful the sanctuary is, how beautiful the décor is. It is about the glory of God. We ought to be concerned about the glory of God, and the ways in which God receives glory. I keep coming back to this point because there are too many of you out there who do not understand this. I am not talking about a selfish thing here. This is a Christ-centered issue. This is what Jesus died for. This is why the Holy Spirit was poured out.[36]

Jesus died on the Cross, poured out the Holy Spirit, and gave us gifts because He wants the Father to receive glory. And likewise, the Father wants to glorify the Son. When we have a service and no one gets healed, and there are no miracles, we may be having a good service from our perspective, but I believe heaven weeps because God is not glorified. The glory of God is not in the house of God. God wants His glory to be present in our midst.

The problem is not on God's part; the problem is on our part because we do not understand. We lack the necessary knowledge of His will that comes to us through His revelatory gifts. It is the Holy Spirit who enables us to know the will of God in our immediate context. As the writer of Proverbs says, "Where there is no vision, the people perish" (Proverbs 29:18, KJV).

---

36. One of the major themes of John 14-17 is relationships: the Father to the Son, the Spirit to the Son, and the relationship of each to the disciples. It is because of what Jesus did that the New Covenant could be enacted and, as a result, the Holy Spirit poured out. The Holy Spirit would be the source of revelatory knowledge of the will of God and also the source of the power to carry out that will. That is why it was good for Jesus to leave the disciples in crucifixion, so that the Spirit, the Parakletos could be poured out. "And I will do whatever you ask in my name, so that the Son may bring ***glory*** to the Father" (John 14:13). The source of our bearing much fruit would be the Holy Spirit. It is this fruit which would bring glory to God. "This is to my Father's ***glory***, that you bear much fruit, showing yourselves to be my disciples" (John 15:8). "He will bring ***glory*** to me by taking from what is mine and making it known to you" (John 16:14).

The story of Jesus changing water into wine[37] gives us a biblical revelation of this truth. "This, the first of his miraculous signs, Jesus performed at Cana in Galilee. He thus revealed his glory, and his disciples put their faith in him" (John 2:11). There it is—Jesus revealed His glory and those who were with Him put their faith in Him. When we have a service with no healings, we have become like a "Nazareth,"[38] a place where there is so little faith for healings and miracles that Jesus is essentially without honor. He is not glorified. We are not going to see people put their faith in God when so little happens in our services. But when we have a service where the glory of God is revealed in the miraculous, we will see an increase in faith in Jesus as Savior, [39] and faith for greater miracles will increase also.

During the Azusa Street Revival there were so many healings taking place that it was difficult not to have faith for miracles. People received faith by being in

37. John 2:1-12.

38. "Jesus left there and went to his hometown, accompanied by his disciples. When the Sabbath came, he began to teach in the synagogue, and many who heard him were amazed. 'Where did this man get these things?' they asked. 'What's this wisdom that has been given him that he even does miracles! Isn't this the carpenter? Isn't this Mary's son and the brother of James, Joseph, Judas and Simon? Aren't his sisters here with us?' And they took offense at him. Jesus said to them, 'Only in his hometown, among his relatives and in his own house is a prophet without honor.' He could not do any miracles there, except lay his hands on a few sick people and heal them. And he was amazed at their lack of faith" (Mark 6:1-6).

39. This seems to be the intent of the apostle John who reveals in his gospel the close connection between Jesus' healings and miracles and the people placing their faith in him. All but one time John uses the word 'sign' in his gospel, which is his word of preference for the healings and miracles of Jesus, and it is connected to people coming to faith in Jesus. Cf. John 2:11, John 2:23, John 3:2, John 4:48.

an atmosphere of the miraculous. We need to contend for the glory of God to be revealed in our churches through miracles and healings, so that the name of Jesus will be held in high honor and He will receive the glory due Him. When this happens, those sitting in the pews will put their faith in Him.

We have too many people in Church who are not putting their faith in God because they have not yet seen His glory revealed. We can scold them and tell them they need to have more faith, but how are they to get that faith? It comes when we say, "God, reveal your glory! Manifest your presence! Heal the sick; perform miracles!" When we contend in this way, then faith is going to come. But it has to start somewhere. It only takes a handful of people contending in faith for faith to come. And when faith comes, the rest will follow.

Mel Tari wrote a book titled *Like a Mighty Wind,*[40] chronicling the revival that swept the island of Timor in 1965. So powerful was this revival that the mighty wind of God continues to blow through Indonesia today. Some years after the publication of this book, Mel was criticized for exaggerating what really happened during the revival. The stories were so amazing that some were having a hard time believing them. The truth is that Mel watered down the stories because he knew that many in the Western Church would not believe what God had done. He knew that if he told the full extent of what God had done, many would write him off as crazy and never read anything about this amazing move of God. How sad.

---

40. Mel Tari, *Like a Mighty Wind* (Green Forest, AR: New Leaf Press, 1971).

CONTEND FOR HIS GLORY!

As the people of God, we are to be concerned for His glory. We are to contend for it! It is so important that we understand that God's supernatural deeds bring glory to Him. Jesus died so that God could be glorified. God anointed Jesus so that He [God] could receive glory. Jesus has anointed us with His Spirit, the Holy Spirit, so that He can receive glory through what we do. This is the "fruit of doing," and it is fruit that will remain. We must be careful not to confuse the fruit of doing in John 14-16[41] with the fruit of *being* that Paul mentions in Galatians 5.[42] The amount of glory God receives is, in some ways, proportionate to how much we believe, how much we will declare, and how much we will decree; how much we will, in obedience, having received revelation, move on that revelation so that miracles take place.[43] We will look more closely at the fruit of doing in a minute.

As believers, we are to do the works of the Kingdom in the name of Jesus. "And I will do whatever you ask in my name, so that the Father may be glorified in the Son. You may ask me for anything in my name, and I

---

41. "I am the vine; you are the branches. If a man remains in me and I in him, he will bear much ***fruit***; apart from me you can *do* nothing" (John 15:5). "This is to my Father's glory, that you bear much ***fruit***, showing yourselves to be my disciples" (John 15:8). "You did not choose me, but I chose you and appointed you to go and bear ***fruit***—***fruit*** that will last. Then the Father will give you whatever you ask in my name" (John 15:16).

42. "But the ***fruit*** of the Spirit is love, joy, peace, patience, kindness, goodness, faithfulness, gentleness and self-control. Against such things there is no law" (Gal. 5:22-23).

43. "It is written: 'I believed; therefore I have spoken.' With that same spirit of faith we also believe and therefore speak" (2 Cor. 4:13). Paul here is quoting Ps. 116:10a.

will do it."[44] Why are we to do the works of the Kingdom in the name of Jesus? In order that the Son can bring glory to the Father. It is for the Father's glory that God wants to answer our prayers and perform the miraculous. Anything less than that means we are robbing God of His glory.

Many of you have heard it said, "touch not the glory of God." There are several ways we can touch the glory of God. For one, we are not to boast in the flesh because the glory belongs to God. The miraculous works that God performs through us in the power of His Holy Spirit are not something we can do in our flesh. They are only possible in the power of His Spirit. When we pray for someone and they get healed, we haven't healed them, God has. We need to be careful to make this distinction when people thank us upon receiving their healing. They can thank us for praying for them, but they need to thank God for healing them.

We can also touch God's glory when we fail to testify to our own healing. When God heals us, His glory is present. Yet many are reluctant to testify to God's healing touch on their own lives for a variety of reasons.

Another way we can touch the glory of God is not to be a people of faith. That actually amounts to stealing from His glory. He makes His glory available to us if we will reach out and receive it in faith. Without faith, we are robbing God of the opportunity to show His glory. The apostle Paul addresses these issues in Romans:

> *I am not ashamed of the gospel, because it is the power of God for the salvation of everyone who believes; first for the Jew, then for the*

---

44. John 14:13-14.

Gentile. For in the gospel a righteousness from God is revealed, a righteousness that is by faith from first to last, just as it is written: "The righteous will live by faith."

Romans 1:16-17

I believe that revelation creates faith and in this atmosphere of faith, miracles happen. I believe God does want to speak today. Not new revelation in the sense of new scripture or new doctrine. I do not mean that at all. But Scripture teaches that God wants to speak to us. God wants us to hear Him. Jesus tells us that the Father is going to take from Him [Jesus] and He is going to reveal it to us.[45] But if we say there is no more revelation, how can He reveal it to us?

He is not going to give us new doctrine, but He is, according to the doctrine already revealed in the Bible, going to give us revelation. Paul said, "It is written: 'I believe; therefore I have spoken.' With that same spirit of faith we also believe and therefore speak . . ." (2 Corinthians 4:13). It is that same spirit of faith.

I have brought you glory on earth by finishing the work you gave me to do. And now, Father, glorify me in your presence with the glory I had with you before the world began.

John 17:4-5

---

45. "'I have much more to say to you, more than you can now bear. But when he, the Spirit of truth, comes, he will guide you into all truth. He will not speak on his own; he will speak only what he hears, and he will tell you what is yet to come. He will bring glory to me by taking from what is mine and making it known to you. All that belongs to the Father is mine. That is why I said the Spirit will take from what is mine and make it known to you'" (John 16:12-15).

Let me ask you a question. Jesus said that He brought God glory on earth by completing the work given to Him to do. Do you believe God has a will for you and for me? And do you believe that in His will for each of us there are some things He wants us to do that will bring glory to His Son, and the Son will bring glory to the Father? I am talking about the "fruit of doing." I am not putting down the fruit of the Spirit as found in Galatians 5. I believe we need to develop godly, biblical character. It keeps us from falling into sin. However, we can have all the character in the world, but if we are not moving in faith for signs and wonders, we are not bringing the glory to God that He desires of us.

Parts of the Church have been deaf to the voice of God and parts of the Church have been blind to the leading of God. But I believe the angels in heaven are excited because they see that we, the Church, are beginning to recapture what was stolen from us. Heaven is excited because the Church is awakening to its divine destiny.

Just as revelation creates faith, so does declaration. Let's look at a passage from John:

> *He [the Father] will bring glory to me [Jesus] by taking from what is mine and making it known to you.*
>
> ***John 16:14-15***

Jesus is saying, "God, my Father, is going to give you information that I have, supernatural revelation, and He is going to make it known to you." Why is that important for believers? When you know what is on the heart of God, you can declare it. And that declaration creates faith in the people that hear it because it is not just your presumption to declare anything you want. You are declaring what you have received through revelation. Some say this is usurping, or seizing without permission, the sovereignty of God, but I disagree. I believe this is learning how to cooperate with the sovereignty of God. When we do not understand how to move with God, to hear from Him, and to believe that He speaks to us today, we are in danger of turning the Bible into a historical book rather than the manual that tells us how to be His disciples.

The Bible is so much more than a historical book. It is not God the Father, God the Son and God the Holy Bible. It is God the Father, God the Son and the God the Holy Spirit. The Holy Spirit breathes and tells us what God is speaking to us. Paul said this, "It is written: 'I believed; therefore I have spoken.' With that same spirit of faith we also believe and therefore speak . . ."[46]

When we hear something from God, or have an impression from God, or we think God is showing us something, then we are to declare it with confidence and heaven will back it up. If you have not heard from God, you will know it, because you will declare something and heaven will not back it up.

GLORIFICATION IS REVELATION AND FAITH TO DO THE WORKS OF THE FATHER

Glorification is the end result of revelation that brings faith. When we talk about glorification, it is important to understand the concept in its fullness. Glorification is the revelation and faith to do the works of God. Within this, the Father's glorification of Jesus is

---

46. 2 Cor. 4:13.

implied. Jesus was glorified by the words and the works the Father gave Him to do.[47] He was glorified not just with words to speak to people, but also with words of instruction that were accompanied by revelation that created the faith that produced the miraculous.

Jesus said, "If I glorify myself, my glory means nothing. My Father, whom you claim as your God, is the one who glorifies me."[48]

When Jesus heard the report that Lazarus was sick, He was actually looking forward to a miracle. He responded by saying, "This sickness will not end in death. No, it is for God's glory so that God's Son may be glorified through it."[49]

At the tomb, Jesus instructs the stone to be rolled away. Distressed, Martha tells Jesus, "'By this time there is a bad odor, for he has been there four days.' Then Jesus said, 'Did I not tell you that if you believe, you will see the glory of God?'"[50]

Oftentimes, hardness of heart brings unbelief even in the midst of the miraculous.

> *Even after Jesus had done all these miraculous signs in their presence, they still would not believe in him. This was to fulfill the word of Isaiah the prophet: "Lord, who has believed our message and to whom has the arm of the Lord been revealed?" For this reason they could not believe, because, as*

47. "I have brought you ***glory*** on earth by completing the work you gave me to do" (John 17:4).

48. John 8:54.

49. John 11:4.

50. John 11:39b-40.

> *Isaiah says elsewhere: "He has blinded their eyes and deadened their hearts, so they can neither see with their eyes, nor understand with their hearts, nor turn—and I would heal them."*
>
> ***John 12:37-40***

The "arm of the Lord" is referring to the strength of God, the power of God. Do you know why it says that God hardened their hearts and deafened their ears? He hardened their hearts after they had hardened their own hearts. Because, to the degree that we receive a revelation and then say "No," it is to that degree that God's judgment will increase in severity. In other words, the greater the revelation you receive and then reject, the greater the consequences.

Likewise, it was out of mercy that Jesus, knowing that they were not going to respond, caused a deafness to come on them. He knew they would not accept Him, and so He removed some of the responsibility by causing their ears to be dulled. This was an act of mercy. It is a demonstration of the mercy of God.

MORE THAN ONE KIND OF FRUIT

Let's now return to the concept of the "fruit of doing." The Father receives glory when we bear much fruit. The Western Church is very concerned with fruit as defined in Galatians 5, and rightly so. The fruit of the Spirit listed in Galatians 5 is love, joy, peace, patience, kindness, goodness, faithfulness, gentleness and self-control. And they are good fruit. I call them the "fruit of being" because these characteristics deal with our state of being; are we being loving, joyous, peaceful, patient, kind, good, faithful, and gentle? But the "fruit of being" is not the only fruit we as believers should be concerned about. We also need to understand the "fruit of doing." It is not an either/or situation. Both are important. We need to understand this distinction because it is important to God.

Jesus spoke about the "fruit of doing" in John 15:8: "This is to my Father's glory, that you bear much fruit, showing yourselves to be my disciples." Jesus is not talking here just about love, joy, peace, patience, kindness, goodness, faithfulness, gentleness and self-control. He is also talking about miracles and healings.

> *I tell you the truth, anyone who has faith in me will do what I have been doing. He will do even greater things than these, because I am going to the Father. And I will do whatever you ask in my name, so that the Son may bring glory to the Father. You may ask me for anything in my name, and I will do it.*
>
> ***John 14:12-14***

In this passage Jesus is telling us that we will perform miracles just as He did, and we will even perform greater miracles than He did! And we will do all of this so that He, Jesus, may bring glory to the Father.

It is so crucial that we understand this passage because this is very important to God. He deserves the glory. Jesus the Son wants to bring glory to His Father whom He loves so much, and He wants to do it through you and me. This is the "fruit of doing." We should not be more concerned about the "fruit of being" than the "fruit of doing." Too many Christians today have been taught to highly value the fruit from Galatians 5 while receiving little or no teaching about the fruit Jesus speaks of in John 14. Jesus cares about the fruit of doing and so should we. We need to learn how to trust and believe, building our faith through revelation so that God will receive the glory through demonstrations of His miracles and healings.[51] And we can do this in the power of the Holy Spirit as we learn to abide in Christ and become repositories of His living Word.

Jesus' high priestly prayer in John 17:10 says, "All I have is yours, and all you have is mine. And glory has come to me through them." Who is the "them" in this verse? It is referring to His disciples! Jesus said that glory was already coming to Him through the disciples because they believed His report. They had already seen that even the demons were subject to Him. All this took place before Pentecost before the Holy Spirit had been poured out. We see Jesus, before Pentecost, receiving glory from the disciples because they are healing the sick and casting out demons.

In John 17:22 Jesus said, "I have given them the glory that you gave me, that they may be one as we

---

51. This truth was revealed in Jesus' own relationship with the Father. Jesus too worked His miracles by revelation from the Father. "'The words I say to you are not just my own. Rather, it is the Father, living in me, who is doing his work. Believe me when I say that I am in the Father and the Father is in me; or at least believe on the evidence of the miracles themselves'" (John 14:10-11). "Jesus replied, 'If anyone loves me, he will obey my teaching. My Father will love him, and we will come to him and make our home with him'" (John 14:23). "'Remain in me, and I will remain in you. No branch can bear fruit by itself; it must remain in the vine. Neither can you bear fruit unless you remain in me. I am the vine; you are the branches. If a man remains in me and I in him, he will bear much fruit; apart from me you can do nothing. If you remain in me and my words remain in you, ask whatever you wish, and it will be given you. This is to my Father's glory, that you bear much fruit, showing yourselves to be my disciples'" (John 15:4-8).

are one." What He is saying here is, "Father, you gave me glory and I have given that same glory to them [the disciples]." This is a delegated authority; it is power that is associated with authority. Again, remember that this is before Pentecost. Jesus said these things before He established the Church.

And then at Pentecost the glory came. The wind and the fire and the miracles came and people believed and were converted. When Peter healed the crippled beggar at the gate called Beautiful, the man then went through the temple, walking and jumping and praising God, and the people were astounded. Peter responds to their astonishment by giving glory to Jesus and to God: "Men of Israel, why does this surprise you? Why do you stare at us as if by our own power or godliness we had made this man walk? The God of Abraham, Isaac and Jacob, the God of our fathers, has glorified his servant Jesus" (Acts 3:12-13).

When Jesus tells us that He has given the glory to us that His Father gave to Him, He is not just talking about giving this glory to the saints, as in the saints in the Roman Catholic Church. Jesus is talking about this glory being given to all who will believe in Him through the Word. The word "saints" as I am using it here is the biblical meaning referring to those who have received the Spirit of God in the new birth.

> *I have given them the glory that you have given me, that they may be one as we are one: I in them and you in me. May they be brought to complete unity to let the world know that you sent me and have loved them even as you have loved me. Father, I want those you have given me to be with me where I am, and to*

see my glory, the glory you have given me because you loved me before the creation of the world.

John 17:22-24

Let me paraphrase these verses: I have communicated to all those who believe—or shall believe in Me—the glorious privilege of becoming sons of God that, being all adopted children of the same Father, they may abide in peace, love and joy in unity. For this reason it is said in Hebrews 2:11, "So Jesus is not ashamed to call them brothers."

Much of the Church has not understood this message, this revelation of what it means to glorify God. I do not say this in judgment, but with sadness. However, I believe that the Church is now coming into the fullness of the knowledge of this message. I believe it will end when His name is glorified here in North America as it is being glorified right now in Latin America, in Asia, and in Africa. I am contending for this.

THE FULL MESSAGE OF THE KINGDOM

When we take off the blinders and see the scriptures clearly, and let the scriptures speak for themselves, we see that we are to have God's power to work miracles. "Christ in you, the hope of glory" is about empowerment for miracles. It is about the message of the Kingdom of God. It is the central message of the Gospel, and it was not meant to be truncated to refer only to the forgiveness of sins. Yes, forgiveness of sins is a part of the message of the Kingdom, but it is not the whole message. The other part of the message is that the Kingdom of heaven is at hand![52]

---

52. "From that time on Jesus began to preach, 'Repent, for the

Therefore, we are to think differently about life, because this power of God is available to us as believers in Christ. We have authority, and the knowledge of this authority will change our way of thinking. That is what it means to repent. The word repent, which is *metanoia* in Greek, literally means "change the way you think."

When we change the way we think, we begin to understand that all things are possible and that nothing is impossible. It is in that moment of revelation that the glory comes, and creative miracles take place in our midst. One of the primary things that keep miracles and healing from happening right now is a lack of expectation.

During the Azusa Street Revival, which marked the beginning of the Pentecostal movement, scores of astounding miracles were recorded.[53] God's great power to heal was revealed and yet many in today's Pentecostal denominations have lost sight of this rich heritage that is theirs. As a result they are no more expectant of miracles than someone raised in a denomination that has not heard of the miraculous.

Let us, the Church, not adhere to doctrine that downplays everything about God's present power for us. We need to stop putting God's power in the past or in the Millennial Kingdom. In 1 Thessalonians 2:12, Paul said "encouraging, comforting and urging you to live lives worthy of God, who calls you into his Kingdom and glory." It does not say "who *will* call you" and it does not say "who *called* you." It says "who *calls* you into His Kingdom and glory." That is a present-tense verb. When I was saved, I

---

kingdom of heaven is near'" (Matt. 4:17).

53. Tommy Welchel and Michelle Griffith, *True Stories of the Miracles of Azusa Street and Beyond* (Shippensburg, PA: Destiny Image, 2013).

was called. When you were saved, you were called into His Kingdom and into His glory. Are we walking in that reality or have we sold our birthright for a pot of porridge called religion?

Are we busy serving the "Great I Was" or the "Great I Will Be" or are we serving the "Great I Am?" When Moses asked God, "Who shall I say has sent me?" God did not say, "Tell them "I Was" sent you, or "I Will" sent you. He said, "Tell them "I Am" has sent me to you" (cf. Exodus 3:14). Hebrews 13:8 says, "Jesus Christ is the same yesterday, today and forever." He has not changed since the time of Moses.

Now God, through the Gospel, wants us to share in the glory of Christ. In 2 Thessalonians 2:14, He is talking about the call, about being saved: "He called you to this through our gospel, that you might share in the glory of our Lord Jesus Christ." We are called to share in that glory! This is a present reality. When you were saved you were called so that you might share in the glory of our Lord Jesus Christ. What a heritage! We are a priesthood of believers, empowered by the Holy Spirit to advance the Kingdom of God so that His glory may be evidenced here and now.

TO LIVE IN THE GOSPEL

We who are called by God are not called just to experience things like feeling good or getting drunk in the Lord. Those are not bad in and of themselves, but there is so much more. Sometimes God gives us experiences for a particular purpose—perhaps to heal us or to prepare us. But in the end, it is not about us. It is not about our experiences. It is about receiving the experience to live a life for His glory.

Luke 9:23 says, "Whoever wants to be my disciple must deny themselves and take up their cross daily and follow me." It is about receiving such power that we might pick up the Cross, the Gospel of Jesus Christ, and do those things that God has told us to do. Often, the world will reject us. Sadly, sometimes the Church will reject us too. Hopefully, it will not be that way forever.

The cross was an instrument associated with suffering. The Gospel is not a gospel that allows us to come and be saved so that we do not have to suffer in the Tribulation. The Gospel is so much more. To live in the Gospel is to experience salvation and the power of God so that we can be faithful in the times of suffering.

Some people say that they do not need the Holy Spirit, or the baptism of the Spirit. They do not think they need to be filled with the Spirit. Now, if you want to operate strictly within the bounds of your own human ability, then you probably will not seek the baptism of the Spirit. If you just want to be a good person, a moral person, and get to heaven, then just His Spirit *in* you is enough. It will bring you salvation but it will not bring glory to God. But if you want to be a believer who brings glory to God, then you are going to need the power of the Holy Spirit *on* you as well as in you, so that you might do those things that only God can do. And *He* gets the glory. Sadly, some unbelievers have more belief than believers. There are some people who are not even committed to Christ but believe in the power to do things.[54]

---

54. In *The Essential Guide to Healing,* coauthored by myself and Bill Johnson I have a chapter dedicated to explaining the development of "unbelieving believers and believing unbelievers." Bill Johnson and Randy Clark, *The Essential Guide to Healing* (Bloomington, MN: Chosen, 2011).

On the Mount of Transfiguration, Jesus experienced the manifested glory in His body, which was to prepare Him for the glory of the Cross. Glory is not just a feeling, and it is not just for healing. Glory is also to prepare us for difficult times of persecution and suffering related to the mission of God.

Please understand, I am not talking here about suffering from disease and sickness. Evangelicals take the passages about suffering and teach that suffering is meant to show a good purpose, and that suffering brings glory. In the Middle Ages the Catholic Church identified holiness with sickness as a way of being purified and sanctified. Unfortunately, it came right over into the Protestant church during the Reformation. This is not a biblical perspective. It is a religious perspective. These suffering passages are dealing with the kind of tribulation and persecution that comes from being a Christian.

I am not referring to suffering from sickness and disease. I am talking about suffering that comes from being faithful to the call of God on your life; it is the persecution that comes, and the rejection that comes. It is about the cost of being a disciple. The Spirit of glory and of God rests upon the persecuted.

> *But rejoice inasmuch as you participate in the sufferings of Christ, so that you may be overjoyed when his glory is revealed. If you are insulted because of the name of Christ, you are blessed, for the Spirit of glory and of God rests on you.*
>
> ***1 Peter 4:13-14***

Hank Hanegraaff says that Pentecostals today are Gnostics. Gnostics were a segment of the early Church that essentially believed that salvation was not found in worship of Christ alone, but also in the psychic process of freeing one's self from the material world via revelation. I believe Hanegraaff says this because he is operating out of a misunderstanding of Pentecostalism.

John's first epistle addresses the dangerous heresy of Gnosticism, which was prevalent in the first two centuries of the Church. (There are passages in this scripture that are dealing with confession of sins and were not written to Gnostics, but to the Christians of the local churches.) This early Gnosticism taught that 'spirit' is entirely good and 'matter' is entirely evil. This is Greek thinking not Hebrew thinking, which holds that the flesh is bad and the spirit is good. The Hebrew belief was that the flesh is good because God created it, and God tells us in Genesis that He is happy with all He has created.[55] This is why we are going to get glorified, resurrected bodies. Our spirit is not just going to be a spirit out there by itself, but a spirit with a glorified body. But because Gnostics believed the flesh was bad, they did not believe in healing. Why would God want to heal your body when all He cares about is your spirit? That is one reason why we ended up with a gospel that focused only on souls being saved and not on healing also.[56] And that is a truncated gospel.

---

55. "God saw all that he had made, and it was very good" (Gen. 1:31a).

56. I am aware that part of this problem of "soul saving" versus the "social gospel" is rooted in the Modernist-Fundamentalist Controversy. There is also Gnostic-type thinking in this division. It is not either/or, either the personal gospel or the social gospel. It should be both/and; both the personal and the social gospel with which the Church should be concerned. The Prophets of the Old Testament and

The true Gospel is that God is not only concerned about my life when I get to heaven. God is concerned about my life right now. God is concerned about all aspects of my life. When we understand the Hebrew way of thinking, we understand that we are living souls, and as living souls, we have a body, soul, and spirit. Our bodies are good. God created our bodies and called them good. So when we have a gospel that is only focused on salvation and not glorification, a gospel not concerned about healing, not concerned about poverty, then we have a truncated gospel, a Gnostic gospel. It is not the full Gospel.

We need to build a culture of faith in the Church today for the miraculous. Praise God that more than tongues happened at Pentecost. I thank God that I have prayed in tongues ever since I was nineteen years old. But for me, it is not about praying in tongues. It is about the power to work miracles. This is the heritage of the Church; these are our roots. We need to go back and re-dig these wells of Abraham, these wells that have been stopped up; because this is our heritage.[57]

I want a hunger to go from the head to the heart of every believer. I want this message of Christ in you, the hope of glory, to go from a concept to a reality. I want us to expect healings and miracles, and I want us, the Church, to build a culture of faith for the miraculous.

When we step into the fullness of the warfare prayer of Jesus, the Lord's Prayer and live in the reality

---

Jesus in Matthew 25, as well as James, give us a strong impetus to be concerned about the social needs of people.

57. This is an analogy to Isaac re-digging the wells of his grandfather Abraham, often used metaphorically for recapturing or re-digging the ancient wells of spiritual power in the past. Cf. Gen. 26:19-22.

of "Thy Kingdom come, thy will be done on earth as it is in heaven," we will see the miraculous and He will be glorified. The Lord's Prayer is such a powerful prayer. Hallowed be God's name! A hallowed name is one that has glory attached to it. Hallowed be Thy name! Glorify Thy name Father, glorify Thy name! Let your kingdom come and your will be done on earth as it is in heaven. Let heaven come to earth! The Kingdom of God is at hand! Sickness and disease are not a part of His Kingdom. They are not God's will.

CHRIST IN YOU, THE HOPE OF GLORY!

We are to live in the fullness of the Gospel. This is our calling. Christ in each one of us is the hope of glory! Christ in us is the hope of miracles! Christ in us is the hope of power! How can we not have expectation for mighty things to happen through us when He is in us and His Spirit is on us?

I think it is much easier to have faith in Jesus than it is to have faith in our faith. We need to believe that He is in us, that He is bubbling up in us, that it is Christ in us, and that He is in us when we begin to get those impressions that He is near, as close as our breath.

We must take our belief beyond those doctrines that have hindered us—those doctrines that have an overemphasis on sovereignty and an overemphasis on holiness. And, can I say it, even an overemphasis on faith. Let Him out! Let Christ out! Believe! Have faith that Christ in you is the hope of glory!

And this is my prayer: that your love may abound more and more in knowledge and depth of insight, so that you may be able to discern what is best and may be pure and blameless until the day of Christ, filled with the fruit of righteousness that comes through Jesus Christ—to the glory and praise of God.

Philippians 1:9-11

THE CORE MESSAGE SERIES

FROM RANDY CLARK

Awed by His Grace / Out of the Bunkhouse

Biblical Basis of Healing

Baptism in the Holy Spirit

Words of Knowledge

Evangelism Unleashed

The Thrill of Victory / The Agony of Defeat

Healing is in the Atonement /
The Power of the Lord's Supper

Open Heaven / Are You Thirsty

Pressing In / Spend and Be Spent

Learning to Minister under the Anointing /
Healing Ministry in your Church

OTHER BOOKS

FROM RANDY CLARK

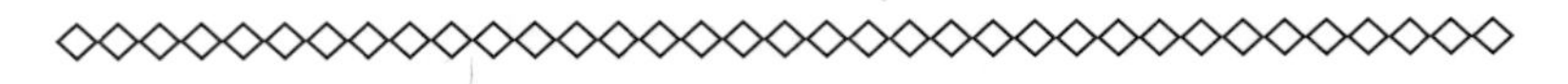

The Essential Guide to Healing

Healing Unplugged

Entertaining Angels

There is More!

Power, Holiness and Evangelism

Lighting Fires

Changed in a Moment

The Healing River and its Contributing Streams

Healing Energy: Whose Energy is It?

TRAINING MANUALS AVAILABLE

Ministry Team Training Manual

Kingdom Foundations Workbook

Empowered Workbook

In "There Is More", Randy will lay a solid biblical foundation for a theology of impartation as well as take a historical look at the impartation and visitation of the Lord in the Church. This will be combined with many personal testimonies of people who have received an impartation throughout the world and what the lasting fruit has been in their lives. You will be taken on journey throughout the world and see for yourself the lasting fruit that is taking place in the harvest field - particularly in Mozambique. This release of power is not only about phenomena of the Holy Spirit, it is about its ultimate effect on evangelism and missions. Your heart will be stirred for more as you read this book.

"This is the book that Randy Clark was born to write."

- Bill Johnson

For this and other books go to: store.globalawakening.com

For a schedule of upcoming events and conferences or to purchase other products from Global Awakening, please visit our website at:
globalawakening.com